# EXMOUTH
## THROUGH TIME
Christopher K. Long

AMBERLEY PUBLISHING

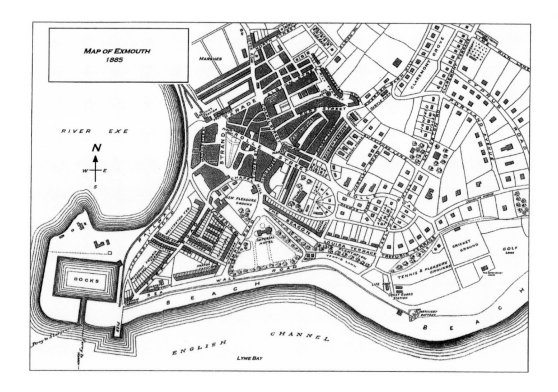

First published 2010
Reprinted 2011

Amberley Publishing
The Hill, Stroud
Gloucestershire, GL5 4EP

www.amberley-books.com

Copyright © Christopher K. Long, 2010

The right of Christopher K. Long to be identified
as the Author of this work has been asserted in
accordance with the Copyrights, Designs and
Patents Act 1988.

ISBN 978 1 84868 334 1

British Library Cataloguing in Publication Data.
A catalogue record for this book is available from
the British Library.

Typeset in 9.5pt on 12pt Celeste.
Typesetting by Amberley Publishing.
Printed in the UK.

# Introduction

*Exmouth Through Time* is the first solo project of local historian and author Christopher Long, who has lived in the town all his life and remembers the more recent changes shown in the book. Christopher has tried to show the changing face of Exmouth, with photographs, slides and postcards of yesteryear compared with the same scenes today.

With an ever growing collection of photographs and information, Christopher wanted to share some of Exmouth's past, and broaden its appeal in this colourful book which helps to visualise the most pivotal changes that have occurred in the town throughout the years.

Reaction to change varies; what some see as an improvement, others see as loss of character. With the town constantly growing and adjusting accordingly, the subtle changes can often go unnoticed. It is hoped that this book will evoke fond memories of the past while showing Exmouth today as a beautiful seaside resort with much to offer.

Christopher has previously co-written three reference books with Maurice Southwell, Elizabeth Gardner and Sally Stocker: *Withycombe Raleigh of Yesteryear* parts one and two (published in 2005); and *Images of England: Exmouth Postcards* (published in 2006).

**Withycombe (Marpool) Mill**
This photograph taken in 1881 shows the author's great grandfather, miller Henry Long at the window of The Withycombe (Marpool) Mill and his wife, Jemima, with sons Fredrick (left) and Henry (right). This long-standing family connection has helped to foster Christopher's passion for the history of the town and local area.

# Acknowledgements

Special thanks go to my wife, Kay, for her help and support throughout this time consuming project, particularly in getting my notes into a format ready for publishing.

I would also like to thank my sons, Jamie, whose help was invaluable in editing the book and Martyn for his photograph of the sunset over the harbour.

Without the kind loan of photographs, and information provided by friends, family and acquaintances over the years, this book would not have been possible. I would particularly like to thank the following people for their help:

The Exmouth Museum, Alan Burgess, Val Clarke, Emma Crane, Tim Edwards, Joan England, Brian Flockhart, Tony Gibson, Malcolm Goodman, Jean Grant, John Hobourn, Lionel Howell, Ian Hitchcock, Albert Johnson, Jo Lee, Shane Luscombe, Jeanne Mallett, Melanie Mock & the RNLI, Ray Moore, Mr and Mrs Pittman, Steve Prowse, Tony Rogers, Philip Rowsell, Harry Sampson, Maurice Southwell, Sally Stocker, David Stoneman, Richard Tarr, Fred Tregay, Mrs Webster, Bob Wilkes and Kim Wyllie.

I also pay tribute to and thank the late Bill Sleeman and Ellen Sparkes.

I would like to dedicate this book to my late cousin, friend and past co-writer Elizabeth Gardner who passed away in August 2008, who is sadly missed by family and friends.

Exmouth Coat of Arms.

CHAPTER 1

# Exmouth Docks

## Harbour Views

When the side of the harbour wall began to collapse on 4 June 1971, the Exe Sailing Clubhouse resembled a capsized boat. The clubhouse was preparing for a party of 100 people when it started to crack and slide towards the water. Luckily, the building was evacuated before it collapsed.

Below – The same area in 2010 – Regatta Court is the latest area of the docks redevelopment to be completed.

The Landing Stage and Launch, Exmouth.

**Steam Ferry**

Taken c. 1925 this photograph shows the Steam Ferry, loaded with passengers on their way to Starcross to meet the connecting Great Western Railway service. This was an alternative route to using the London and South West Railway link line to Exeter. The Pavilion building, pictured behind the waiting passengers, provided entertainment until it was demolished in the 1950s.

Below – The area today is still used for the Exmouth to Starcross ferry, which runs regularly through the summer months.

THE BOAT HOUSES, EXMOUTH

**The Boat Houses**

Taken *c.* 1946 this postcard shows a few of the ninety-nine boat houses and chalets of Shelly Beach that edged the dock basin. Through the 1990s these houses were demolished to make way for the regeneration of the docks area, with the last two chalets being taken down in 2002.

Below – Taken during a trip on the *Pride of Exmouth* pleasure cruiser in 2009, it is easy to see how much this area has altered.

**The Docks**

This photograph, taken in the summer of 1989, shows the working nature of the docks before its closure on 31 December of that year. Note the grain silos, piles of scrap metal, loading cranes and fishing equipment, all evidence of the industrial use of the docks.

Below – Today, in total contrast, the New England style housing and up-to-date marina lift-bridge make it an attractive feature of the town.

**Exmouth Pier**

Exmouth's wooden pier *c.* 1920 was used as a boarding station by the Devon Dock, Pier & Steamship Company. The *Duchess of Devonshire*, pictured, was one of the two paddle steamers used by the company for trips to Torquay, Brixham, Dartmouth, Sidmouth and Weymouth. Sadly, she was wrecked at Sidmouth on 27 August 1934.

Below – Today a similar service is offered by Stuart Line Cruises and their *Pride of Exmouth* pleasure cruiser can be seen at the pier.

### Celebrations in the Docks

The naming ceremony, held in the Exmouth Docks, for the new Trent Class lifeboat *Forward Birmingham* on 20 September 1996 was a popular event, with the Marine Band adding to the excitement.

Below – The warehouses behind the onlookers in the top photograph were replaced by the first residential properties built on the developing marina. The Beachcomber Bar, to the right of the photograph, helps to identify how the area has changed.

**Docks Entrance**

This view of the docks entrance, with Dawlish Warren beyond, was taken from the dock basin *c.* 1989. The swing bridge, to the right of the photograph, is open ready for passing boats.

Below – Taken in September 2009, the newly completed Regatta Court apartment complex stands where the final chalets of Shelly Beach once stood.

## Wilson's Quay

Wilson & Son Timber Company can be seen to the left of this photograph taken in the 1950s. The gentlemen pictured are stood at the end of Wilson's Quay looking into the entrance of the docks. The chalets of Shelly Beach can be seen on the far side of the docks; notice the slipway into the dock basin.

Below – The same area in June 2010 basking in the summer sun.

## Docks Through Time

One of the most dramatic changes to Exmouth in recent years is the regeneration of the docks area, making it the ideal front cover for this book. The boat pictured in the top photograph, taken *c.* 1971, is the German built coaster *Kerstin-Eva*. Ships like this were regular visitors to the commercial docks.

Below – Taken during the spring of 2010 this photograph shows why Exmouth is so popular with visitors. The pathway around the marina is lit at night making it perfect for an evening stroll.

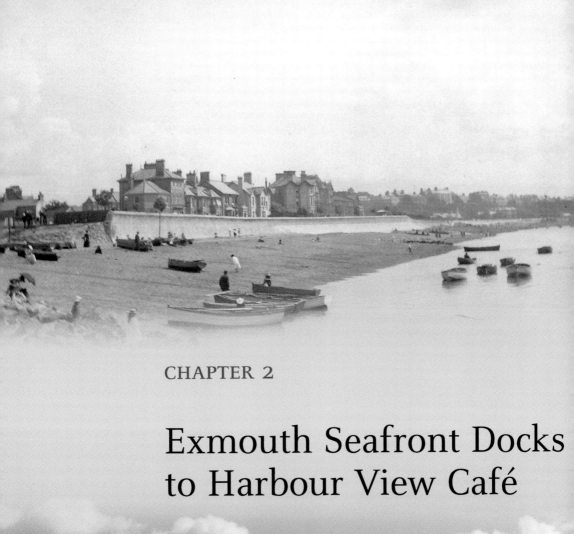

CHAPTER 2

# Exmouth Seafront Docks
# to Harbour View Café

The Beach, Exmouth.

## The Seafront

Even in this 1912 postcard, the photographer used artistic licence to create an image of a busy seafront. The giveaway is that the people in the foreground aren't to scale. An insightful photograph of the time with bathing huts on the beach and gas lighting.

Below – In 2006 major under-pinning work to the sea wall created a construction site on the beach.

## The Esplanade

Do you notice anything missing from the hand-painted photograph taken pre-1897? The absence of the clock tower, erected as a memorial to Queen Victoria's Diamond Jubilee in 1897, indicates that the image is older than the colour suggests.

Below – The clock tower can be seen in this picture *c.* 1950. Both photographs show the Esplanade towards the old Pier with the beautiful Exe Estuary and Haldon Hills beyond.

F_41508. EXMOUTH: BEACH GARDENS & PROMENADE.

Beach Gardens

These smartly dressed people and the bathing huts on the beach help to date this picture
c. 1906.

   Below – The formal gardens, with shrubs and herbaceous borders have been replaced by
The Octagon shop and Torbay Palms. The round, green Allen Williams steel machine gun
turret, seen here in front of the Octagon, was used during the Second World War to shoot
at enemy planes on their way up the river to bomb Exeter.

### The Deer Leap

Public houses often change their name and Exmouth's seafront bar is no exception.

Below – Formerly called The Deer Leap, The Bath House is now more in keeping with its original history. In the 1790s, Dr Black established a bathhouse with hot or cold saltwater, said to cure all sorts of ailments and to re-invigorate the visitor.

The Bowling Green

What better way to while away the hours than a game of bowls while watching the sea and the passing ships? Opened in 1912, there were two bowling greens on the seafront. According to the Exmouth guide book of 1932, an hour-long game of bowls cost three-pence.

Below – The carpet bed of 80,000 plants was transported to Exmouth seafront from London's Trafalgar Square in August 2005, after spending only one day promoting a wine festival.

## Exmouth Promenade

Exmouth Promenade has always been a popular trip for Sunday afternoon drives, due to the two miles of sea views. Can you spot your old motor among those pictured in these postcards? There's a good selection of the cars of the time including: 1950s – Standard Super 10, Austin A40, Austin A30 and Below – 1960s Morris Minor, Volvo, Austin A55, Vauxhall, Ford Anglia, Caravelle, Minis and Ford Zephyr.

Royal Beacon Hotel

This spectacular view taken from a hand-painted lithographic print *c.* 1830 would have been what drew visitors to stay at Exmouth's Royal Beacon Hotel. Constructed in 1810 as The Marine Hotel, the proprietor changed its name to The Royal Beacon in 1844, following a visit from the King of Saxony.

Below – The views are still as magnificent from the Royal Beacon Hotel today.

## Outdoor Swimming Pool

This postcard shows the swimming pool on Exmouth seafront not long after it opened in 1932. It closed c. 1985 following the opening of the indoor swimming pool and sports centre in town.

Below – This prime site on the Exmouth promenade remained undeveloped until recently when construction of the eagerly awaited entertainment complex began. Unfortunately, progress on this building has been delayed and is unlikely to be completed in 2010 as hoped.

**Exmouth Beach**

Holiday-makers enjoying Exmouth beach *c.* 1934. The sea wall in front of the grand seafront buildings was designed by John Smeaton and constructed in 1842.

Below – the crew of Exmouth Inshore Lifeboat returning to the former lifeboat station in 2006. Familiar to many couples, the 'Abode of Love' to the left of the photograph, provides a sheltered station for enjoying the view and each other's company.

CHAPTER 3

# From Boating Lake to Orcombe Point

## Coastguard Station

The coastguard station and cottages shown on the right of this photograph were built in the 1820s to help combat smuggling, which was rife along the Devon coastline at that time. Their prime position on the seafront meant that the crew were ready to spring into action using their aptly named Revenue Cutter boat *The Nimble*.

Below – Today, the boating lake and leisure grounds have replaced the coastguard station and cottages, which were demolished in the 1950s.

## Seafront Transport

This First World War tank was a feature on the Exmouth seafront for a period between the wars. The former Lifeboat Station can be seen behind the tank in this photograph taken *c.* 1920.

Below – A more recent attraction to the seafront is the Carriage Café, which was added as a feature to the Model Railway Museum in March 2007.

Inset – The carriage prior to being moved to its current position.

## Lifeboats

Photographed outside the former Lifeboat Station in 1933 Exmouth's first motorised lifeboat *Catherine Harriet Eaton* with her crew. The newly acquired lifeboat was fitted with a 35 hp engine and capable of reaching speeds of 7 knots.

Below – Using the new ramp and launch tractor the current lifeboat *Margaret Jean* is seen here returning from a practice exercise in May 2010. A type 12-21, she is the latest in lifeboat technology.

## Shipwrecks

On 10 October 1907 in the aftermath of high seas and gale force winds, the wreckage of Russian cargo schooner *Tehwila* can be seen strewn across the beach at Orcombe Point. Luckily all the crew were rescued.

Below – On 20 September 2006 the yacht *Ambition* was washed up on the beach. All three crew members were rescued by the RNLI but the following day *Ambition* suffered the same fate as *Tehwila* when she was totally wrecked by rough seas.

## Queens Drive

When this postcard was sent in 1912, there was no sign of the busy highway that is Queens Drive today. The coastguard cottages, former lifeboat station and tower of the Harbour View can be seen to the right of the photograph.

Below – Taken from the same point but in the opposite direction, this 1960s photograph shows how the area has changed with the addition of beach huts and a road. Note how low the sand dunes are.

**Marine Drive**

Marine Drive to Orcombe Point in the 1920s. The charabanc was the link between the railway station and hotels/guest houses in Exmouth at that time.

Below – This spectacular early evening view of Exmouth beach, looking towards Orcombe Point, shows one of the many reasons why it is such a popular tourist destination.

### Orcombe Café

What a welcome sight the Orcombe Café made at the end of the two-mile stroll along the beach or a blustery walk in the rain! The reward of a coffee and cake, while taking in the spectacular view of the sea, provided enough sustenance to make the return trip. The café was taken down *c.* 1992.

Below – Today this picnic platform area is enhanced by flags, designed by Exmouth Community College students to mark the start of the Jurassic Coast.

### Sand Dunes and Maer

Taken in 1959, looking from the east of the beach towards the mouth of the Exe, this lovely panoramic view shows the sand dunes and open space of the Maer. The Haldon Hills can be seen across the water and the only structures on the landscape are the beach huts lining the road.

Below – Taken in 2010 the changes to the area include the addition of the RNLI station.

Inset – the same view c. 1900 before Queen's Drive was constructed.

Orcombe Point, looking West, Exmouth.

5.571

## Orcombe Point

Looking from the cliffs towards Orcombe Point, Rodney Bay can be seen in the foreground with Exmouth beach in the near distance.

Below – The Geo-needle Obelisk placed on top of these cliffs was unveiled by HRH Prince of Wales on 3 October 2002 to inaugurate the start of the Jurassic Coastline World Heritage Site. This structure was the creation of artist and sculptor Michael Fairfax. It stands five metres tall and is embedded with the nine different rock types found along the Jurassic Coast.

CHAPTER 4

# Withycombe Raleigh

## Exmouth to Budleigh Salterton Railway Line

Due to Dr Beeching's cutbacks, the railway line from Exmouth to Budleigh Salterton was closed in 1967. This link went along the old viaduct at the bottom of Marpool Hill, through Littleham Cross and onto Budleigh Salterton. The viaduct, however, remained a feature of the Withycombe landscape until it was demolished *c.* 1985.

Below – Today houses have been built on the site and much of the old railway line is used as a cycle track and path.

## Marpool Hall

Marpool Hall, stood at the top of Phear Park drive, prior to being demolished in 1951. The Phear Family gave the 8.5 acre park to the town in 1909.

Below – Today the bowling club stands on the site where the Hall once stood. The park now offers pitch and putt, tennis courts, a mini golf course, and a play park as well as attractive parkland.

## Withycombe Mill

One of the earliest colour pictures of Withycombe's (Marpool) Mill shows faithful employee, Frank Bastin when the mill wheel was still in operation. In 1962 the mill was demolished to make way for the flood relief channel, following the severe flooding of 1960.

Inset – Inside the mill.

Below – The mill wheel, given to the town by miller, Harry Long, now forms the centre piece of an attractive water feature found just outside the gate of the Imperial Hotel on Bath Road.

### Withycombe Village Road

Taken in 1961, looking down Withycombe Village Road, the Mill Cottages can be seen on the left with the mill building behind.

Below – The same area today has changed greatly, the cedar tree and wall of Exmouth Community College to the left of the picture help to visualise the changes.

**Bowyers Bakery**

The memory of Bowyers Bakery is probably one of the better ones shared by many ex-pupils of Exmouth Comprehensive School. The choice of whether to have the Sputnik (mock cream cake) or a quarter pound of sweets from the huge variety on display was difficult.

Below – Today the former bakery has been converted into flats and The Granary opened, which still proves a popular haunt for many children on the way home from school.

The Village, Withycombe

## The Holly Tree Inn

The Holly Tree Inn and adjoining saddlery business were both under the ownership of the Stocker family when this image was captured *c.* 1914; the inn still remains but, the saddlery was demolished *c.* 1940.

Below – There is still a holly tree in front of the public house today, although it is a sapling from the original tree, which gave the inn its name.

## Jubilee Terrace

The Jubilee Terrace area of Withycombe Village, is seen here before the road widening scheme in 1967. Part of the burial ground in front of the Withycombe Raleigh C of E school was used to make way for the new road. The Moorfield Dairy and neighbouring cottages, seen behind the brick wall, were also demolished to relieve the bottleneck.

Below – Enough space was created to provide the paths and parking bays, which help to ease congestion today.

## Country House Inn

Built in 1887 as part of Jubilee Terrace, the Country House was originally a blacksmith's and cider house. This photograph was taken in 1976 when Leonard "Roy" and Joan Burgess were landlord and landlady, before the extension into the house next door.

Below – Taken in July 2010 on a beautiful summer's evening.

### Cemetery Place

On the junction of Withycombe Village Road and Pound Lane, just behind Greengate Cottages, there was a walled in and overgrown graveyard which belonged to the Plymouth Brethren.

Below – Today the area is used as a grass rest area after being cleared and opened up to the public in the 1980s. The only sign of its former use are the gravestones around the walled edge.

Inset – An Edwardian photograph of Cemetery Place now known as Sunny View Cottages.

# CHAPTER 5

# Littleham Village

### Littleham Village Road

Looking from Littleham Village Road towards the junction at Littleham Cross *c.* 1930. The Lloyds Bank building to the left of the photograph has changed little, although it is now the Post Office. The Cranford Hotel, later the Cranford Tavern, can be seen to the right of the road before it was burned down in 1993.

Inset – Cranford Tavern after the fire.

Below – The site was later developed into Orcombe Point residental flat.

46

## Stationmaster's House

The stationmaster's house at Littleham Cross was on the Exmouth to Budleigh Salterton line. At the time of its closure, the railway track had only been in operation for sixty-four years. The pretty route gave the option of catching the London train from Tipton St John rather than having to go into Exeter.

Below – The cream building is the old stationmaster's house, taken from a slightly different angle, with the bungalows of Jarvis Close behind.

### Brook Cottages

This photograph shows Brook Cottages in Castle Lane, Littleham Village *c.* 1900.

Below – They were demolished in the 1930s and the area is now used for parking with ornamental trees and a shrubbery area. Around the time of the Napoleonic War this area, adjacent to the Littleham Church, was well known as a smugglers' haunt where booty was reputedly hidden in the graveyard.

## Littleham Village

The chocolate box charm of Littleham Village can be seen in this hand-painted postcard sent in 1938. The thatched cottages can be seen to the right of the church and this quaint Devon scene shows the villagers happily posing for the picture.

Below – With the cottages now gone, the villagers keep the charm of the village alive by producing beautiful flower displays for the annual 'Britain in Bloom' competition.

**Tythe College**

This winter view of Tythe Cottage, Littleham *c.* 1900, shows one of the few remaining thatched cottages in the village.

Below – Once a church property thought to date from the fifteenth century, now a restaurant and tearooms which come alive every summer with an abundance of flowers and holiday-makers enjoying a Devon Cream Tea.

## Holiday Camp

This view of the holiday camp at Westdown Farm, Sandy Bay taken in the 1930s shows the early beginnings of what is now reputed to be one of the largest holiday camps in Europe. The first visitors to this lovely spot would have shared their field with grazing sheep and purchased fresh milk and eggs from the farmer.

Below – A far cry from the antiquated caravans in the first picture, the new luxurious mobile homes today offer comfort, warmth and plenty of space.

## Straight Point

Taken from Straight Point *c.* 1934 this view shows much of the area that now forms the 300 acre site of the Haven flagship, Devon Cliffs Holiday Park. It is easy to see why it became so popular, with its beautiful Devon countryside and sandy beaches.

Below – The beach of Sandy Bay looking towards Straight Point. Sun, sea and sand, British summertime at its best.

## Sandy Bay Beach

Another stunning view of Sandy Bay beach, this time looking towards Orcombe Point *c.* 1958.

Below – The steep steps have now been replaced by a slope, creating improved access for visitors, emergency vehicles and the tractor which keeps the beach clean.

## The Club House

This image of the old Club House at Sandy Bay holiday camp was taken from a postcard that was sent to Exeter in 1968. It just goes to show that not everyone travelled a long way to go on holiday in the 1960s.

Below – The Spa, swimming pool and club house building, one of the many entertainment complexes that visitors can enjoy at the holiday park today. How things have changed!

CHAPTER 6

# Exmouth Town Centre

**The Parade**

Looking along the Parade from Exeter Road this photograph, taken in August 1938, shows the area during a flood caused by heavy rainfall and high tides. The steps and high pavements to the right of this picture prevented flood water entering the shops. The buildings behind the horse and cart, known as the Staples buildings, were demolished as part of the redevelopment of the area after the Second World War.

Below – The Parade in 2010, now a modern shopping area.

## Woolworths and Iceland

It was the end of an era on 6 January 2009, as the Woolworths store on the Parade closed its doors for the last time. A retreat for parents in town on a wet day with sweets and toys to keep the children happy, it will be sorely missed.

Below – Iceland moved into the vacated shop opened to the public on 20 August 2009.

Exeter Road

Taken in 1876, looking down Exeter Road from the Parade. Mona Island, which was formerly known as Pratteshide, can be seen to the centre of this picture. In the thirteenth century, the area was marshy and tidal and Mona Island was used as a landing quay for the Exmouth to Starcross ferry service. The draining and reclamation work to the estuary area started in 1811, making it possible to develop Exeter Road and the Colony area.

Below – Exeter Road in 2010.

## London Residential & Commercial Hotel

The London Residential & Commercial Hotel during demolition in 1964. Built *c.* 1800 it was originally used as a coaching inn by horse-drawn coach travellers taking the route from Exmouth to Exeter. It was situated to the left of the site currently occupied by Blockbuster.

Below – The crane is parked in the London Inn car park whilst installing the large clock on the Tempest building in 2006.

## Chapel Street

Chapel Street in 1964 showing the Forester's Arms on the left and The Volunteer on the right of the picture. Porky Down, the butcher, is still located in the same premises. Hodges men's outfitters can be seen on the corner of the Parade where Warrens Bakery is today.

Below – The busy Magnolia Shopping Centre in 2010.

**The Strand**

The Strand, pictured in 1895, looking towards the corner where it meets Victoria Road. These beautiful Victorian shop buildings suffered during the heavy bombing of the town on the 26 February 1943, when twenty-five people were killed and forty injured.

Below – The Wiltshire and Dorset Bank building survived and is now the premises of Lloyds TSB.

### The Strand

Taken prior to the buildings being demolished to make way for Victoria Road in 1897, this scene shows the corner of the Strand with Thomas' ironmonger's to the left displaying a kettle above its entrance. The boarded up building to the right was once Exmouth's main Post Office.

Below – The same area in 2010 with Garner's Home Hardware now occupying the site of the original ironmonger's, having taken over from Hancock and Wheeler in 2000.

**Lennard's Bar**

Leonards Bar, originally established by Reg Lennard in 1955, remained in the family until his son Bruce retired in 1999. Following some refurbishment it reopened as Malloy's.

Below – In 2004 the premises changed its name to The Clipper, recognising its link to the buildings former use as a tea warehouse during the late eighteenth Century. Their sign, on the front of the building, shows a Tea Clipper.

## The Strand Gardens

Dating early 1870s this view shows the newly formed Strand Gardens as displayed in a tourist guidebook of the time. The Victorian grandeur portrayed would have been sure to entice wealthy visitors. The land was donated to the town by Lord Rolle following the demolition of Market House and The Globe Hotel to make way for the beginning of Rolle Street.

Below – The Strand Gardens in 2008, prior to current redevelopment work, which is due for completion 2010.

### Rolle Street

The Strand end of Rolle Street *c.* 1900, this image shows a bustling Victorian shopping scene. The grand architecture, gas lamps and alcoves were befitting as this was Exmouth's Town Hall (picture from Bill Sleeman's collection).

Below – During the Strand redevelopment works in 2010, although the architecture remains unchanged the feel is somewhat different, with the awnings gone and the Savoy cinema in the old Town Hall building.

**Tower Street Methodist Church**

The demolition of these town houses in Queen Street *c.* 1964, must have improved the natural light in the Tower Street Methodist church.

Below – Today the area is used as a much needed church car park. Changes such as these often go unnoticed and unrecorded but contribute to the ever-changing face of the town.

Inset – Front view of Tower Street Methodist Church *c.* 1900.

CHAPTER 7

# Exmouth Town

### Exmouth Celebrations

Exmouth's first railway station and railway line to Exeter were opened during a grand ceremony on 1 May 1861. The cost of bringing this link to Exmouth was £86,000, a considerable sum for the time. The gable end building to the right of the station is the South Western, now the Strand public house.

Below – This same building can be seen behind the Royal Marine Band as they marched in May 2007 for the 25th Anniversary Parade remembering the liberation of the Falkland Islands.

### Exmouth Railway Station

This impressive building replaced the original railway station in 1926. It was demolished in January 1980 to make way for the town's relief road and roundabout.

Below – The third and current railway station, opened in 1976. Lacking the grandeur of its predecessor it is located approximately 300 feet north of where the second station was situated.

### St Saviour's Church

St Saviour's Church on Church Street opened as a mission chapel in 1881. It closed in 1988.

Below – The Open Door Centre now stands on the site, continuing to offer Christian support to those who need it. The hall is also used for various meetings including Sue Coleman's Saturday morning Weight Watchers session, some of her group are pictured here in March 2010.

### The Stand

This Victorian postcard dating *c.* 1900 (from Bill Sleeman's collection) shows the view from the corner of The Strand looking toward Chapel Hill.

Below – The same view today. The former Thomas Tucker building appears to be the only one to have stood the test of time; the other buildings have either been replaced or altered. The area is currently affected by The Strand redevelopment scheme.

### Holman and Ham Chemist's

Looking from where the Town Hall is today, this picture of Holman & Ham Chemist's was taken in the 1920s. Established in the eighteenth century, the chemists moved to the current building when the original one was replaced in the 1930s.

Below – When the chemist stopped dispensing in the 1980s the aptly named Remedies Bar was opened. Remedies has since been replaced by Prezzo pizzeria.

2109. MANOR GROUNDS, EXMOUTH.

## Manor Gardens

Previously the grounds of the old Manor House, which stood on Chapel Hill, the Manor Gardens opened to the public in 1896. Over the years these beautiful gardens have benefited from three different bandstands.

Below – The current bandstand is used to full benefit during the Exmouth Festival fortnight in May. Renaissance Ladies Barbershop singers are shown here during the 2009 festival.

### The Pilot Inn

Taken from a glass slide this image shows Chapel Hill *c.* 1897. The Pilot Inn was once situated next to the Holy Trinity Chapel, which stood roughly where the roundabout is today. At that time The Pilot Inn was called Chapel House Inn, but changed its name following the chapel's demolition in 1827.

Below – The Pilot Inn 2010 is the only recognisable landmark from the earlier image. The roundabout is enhanced by a fountain and wonderful flower displays.

## High Street

This postcard shows the newly created High Street, *c.* 1897 (from Bill Sleeman's collection). Following the creation of Rolle Street in 1875, Chapel Street was divided into two areas. The bottom end remained as Chapel Street, better known today as the Magnolia Centre, and the top renamed High Street.

Below – High Street today with the popular Heavitree public house on the left.

**Beacon Hill**

The Beacon Hill area, *c.* 1900 has seen little change. The Assembly Rooms, seen to the left with a handcart outside, played a major role in attracting Georgian gentry to the town as a fashionable meeting place in the 1790s. The town became popular around this time as travel to the continent was restricted due to the Napoleonic Wars.

Inset – The Imperial Hotel from the seafront.

Below – The Imperial Hotel in 2010, built in 1869, can be seen to the right of the picture.

CHAPTER 8

# Outskirts of Exmouth

### Brixington Farmhouse

Brixington Farmhouse pictured in the 1960s, during its renovation into the Farmhouse public house. The surrounding farmland later became the Brixington housing estate and shopping parade.

Below – The Farmhouse is popular today for family food and sports coverage; the flags are out to support England in the 2010 FIFA World Cup that was being held in South Africa.

## Bystock Gate Lodge

This photograph shows Bystock Gate Lodge in its original position at the bottom of Bystock Drive where it joined with St John's Road. It was moved c. 1993 to make way for the continuation of the Dinan Way relief road. It was taken down and rebuilt in its current location further up the drive.

Below – The extended and renovated Bystock Gate Lodge is now located closer to Bystock House.

**Bystock House**

During its renovation, Bystock House was gutted by fire on 14 March 1906. The blaze was so large that it was attended by the Exmouth and Exeter Fire Brigades. The house was completely rebuilt following the fire.

Below – Bystock House, following a rare snowfall in January 2010, is now run by Devon Sheltered Homes Trust which offers accommodation for forty-one residents.

## A La Ronde

A La Ronde with a thatched roof before it was replaced *c.* 1890. This unique house was completed in 1798 for Jane Parminter and her cousin Mary, following their European tour. Taken over by the National Trust in 1991 it is situated off Summer Lane.

Below – A La Ronde in 2007, little has changed over the years, the tiled roof with its dormer windows and catwalk are the only noticeable changes.

## Point-in-View Church

The Point-in-View Church was built in the grounds of A La Ronde as a private chapel for Jane and Mary Parminter. It was completed in the summer of 1811, the same year as Jane Parminter passed away. It had its own pastor, who lived in the Manse House which can be seen in this photograph to the left of the church.

Below – The church today is open to visitors for private devotion, holds weekly services and is licensed for marriages.

## St John in the Wilderness Church

This print shows St John in the Wilderness Church *c.* 1840. It was built between 1385 and 1435 and is believed to be on the site of an ancient Saxon church.

Below – Today the church is a beautiful setting for weddings. In 1912, however, it was discovered that marriages conducted in the church from 1886 were not legal. This was rectified in 1912 by an Order in Council. The church was not relicensed for marriages until the 1970s.

**Dalditch Royal Marine Camp**

Dalditch Royal Marine Camp on Woodbury Common in 1945, during the last days of the Second World War. In June 1944 around 5,000 troops were encamped at Dalditch awaiting their involvement in the D-day landings.

Inset – Private Ron Webster at Dalditch camp.

Below – Fred Tregay, who took part in the D-day invasion, shows the area where the guardroom would have been during his basic training at Dalditch in 1942. One of the buildings is still present and used as a bat hibernacula.

## Pine Ridge Café

The Pine Ridge Café at the top of Higher Marley Road, pictured *c.* 1960. Offering light refreshments, it was popular with both locals and visitors but sadly fell into disrepair after it closed.

Below – Although the building has been restored to its former glory it is no longer open to the general public.

## Blackhill Quarry

This rare image of Blackhill Quarry was taken in the 1930s, when pebbles were extracted, sieved and hammered by hand to form material for roads. The quarry extracts from the pebble bed formation of Woodbury Common, which is thought to date back to the Triassic Age.

Below – Current operators use sophisticated processes and plant to produce sand and aggregates for use in building construction and roads.

# CHAPTER 9

# Exmouth People

## Exmouth Characters

Bill Sleeman (left) and Garth Gibson (right) were two prominent Exmouth figures who will be sadly missed. Local historian and author, Bill, passed away 31 August 2009. He was Chairman of Exmouth Museum and a key figure of Exmouth's RNLI and many of the town's clubs. Exmouth's first Town Crier, Garth, passed away 20 May 2009. His love of people and sense of fun made him popular, which was evident when so many lined the funeral route as Garth's horse-drawn hearse made its way to the church.

**Exmouth Youth Camp**

The cast of Exmouth's youth group, 14–20s Music and Drama Society, pictured following their performance of 'Calamity Jane' in 1974.

Below – Renamed Centre Stage in 1991, this rare photograph shows the cast of 'My Fair Lady' with the full company and production team of the show in October 2008. The Society will start to celebrate forty years of entertainment with an Anniversary Ball in November 2010 and the year will close with a week of Anniversary Concerts in October 2011.

**Brixington Blues**

Brixington Blues Under 16s were Champions of the Taunton Youth League in 2000/01. Back (left to right): Chris Fereday, David Radford, Will Bennett, Martin Rice, David Hitchcock, Tim Thorn, Steven Hack, Robert Hall and Phil Taylor. Front Row: Danny Potter, Tony Pallet, Ian Corrick, James Perkins, Leigh Wright, Gareth Wicks.

Below – Brixington Blues Under 16s football team in 2009/10 won both the Juventus League and Juventus Knockout Cup. Back (left to right): Dan Fulls, James Flockhart, Josh Jones, Alex Sparkes, Manager – Bryan Flockhart, Josh Bray, Peter Rundle, Luke Spray, Sam Wells. Front: Sam Dickinson, Alex Coull, Matt Skinner, Karl Riddell, Tom Taylor, Callum Shipton and Adam Otto.

**Royal Mail Staff**

Exmouth Royal Mail delivery staff in July 1973. From left to right: Joe Oldham, Cyril Stone, Tony Trivett, Fred Wilkinson,Tom Pritchard, Bill Skinner, Denis Webb, Gerry Marriott, Glyn Marshman, Derek Philips, Charlie Collard, Stan Marshall, Alan Palmer. Kneeling: Ron Davey, Philip (Twinkle) Quick, Harry Burden, John Macmillan. Standing: Len Carder, Tony Webb, Keith Milford, Geoff Gould.

Below – A group of Exmouth Royal Mail delivery staff in May 2010: Ian Nottingham, Mick Ingram, Tim Clatworthy, Daniel Wood, Pete Brown, Christopher Long, John Hawkins, Paul Smith, Geoffrey Williams and Bernice Williams.

Cricket Teams

Exmouth and Withycombe Cricket Club members in 1946. Back (left to right): A Swanson (Capt.), A. Abbott, S. Bryant, H. Lunn, J. Sanders, G. Elson, W. Bettison, B. Fudge, E. Ware, P. Tonks. Middle: Mr Buttle, L. Poole, B. Curtis, W. L. Birch, F. Farrant, M. Stephens, W. Reynolds, K. Alford. Front: A. Bright. S. Fudge, E. Hall, F. Rogers, J. Perry, C. King.

Below – As Devon Champions, Exmouth Cricket Club in 2003. Back: S. Gardner, M. Sampson, M. Woodman, J. Kavenagh, J. Tozer, B. Thompson, J-P Duminy (who has since played for South Africa), D. Court. Front: M. (Dickie) Davis, J. Page (Capt.) and T. Wright.

## Theatre Groups

The cast of Exmouth Amateur Operatic Society during the production of 'The White Horse Inn' in 1988.

Below – Renamed the Exmouth Amateur Musical Theatre Company on 29 November 2007, members are pictured during the Company's Centenary celebrations in March 2010. Back (l-r): Paul Caygill, Ben Martin, Lance Vernon, Mark Smith, Hugh Chudley, Mike Kilbran, Anthony Lees, Daniel Thorogood, Phill Killoran, Craig Butler, Ian Taylor, Glenda Budd, Julie Parker. Middle: Rosie Bing, Alison Walker, Anita Smith, Lorna Bryant, Helen Rushton, Sue Sellek, Anne Killoran, Rachel Hodge, Michelle Chudley, Jayne Thorogood, Kara Leaworthy, Annabel Youldon, Charlie Mackay, Ann Bradley, Gaye Caygill, Emma Mackay. Front: Rachel Worsley, Clare Philbrock, Debra Butler, Lynne Caygill, Ken Sellek, Val Clarke, Caroline Fegan, Allen Simkin, Kate Lees, Kirsty Sydenham, Jo Killoran and Sarah Reed.

Lifeboat Crew

The crew of the *Catherine Harriet Eaton* posing in front of their new lifeboat in 1933.

Below – The official photograph taken by Mike Powell, on 20 November 2009, when the new lifeboat station was granted operational status. On the lifeboat (left to right): D. Perkin, Coxswain/Mechanic – T. Mock, M. Sansom, A. Carey, S. Ranft, S. Hockings-Thompson, Kneeling; G. White. Standing: N. Pearce, M. Cockman, S. Satchell, A. Smith, A. Stott, R. Jackson, R. Vines, I. Taylor, G. Munnings, T. Angell, Dr C. May, K. Riley, P. Thomas, D. Jackman, C. Sims, N. Hurlock, D. Page, P. Renouf, D. Hodgkinson, D. Preece, H. Saunders, R. Thompson, J. Haynes, D. Ashman, R. Kathro and M. Newton.

**Fire Brigade Crews**
The Exmouth Urban District Council Fire Brigade proudly stand by their new fire engine in 1941, pictured to the left are local officials.

   Below – Exmouth Fire crews in 2010 (left to right): Watch Commander – Stefan (Nobby) Clark, Matthew (Matty) Harper, Crew Commander – Stephen Johncock, (Dangerous) David Hill, Lyndon Mason, Gregory Rowland, Station Manager – Andy Hallam, Ryan Draper, Paul Ash and Richard (Hoppy) Hopkins.

## Exmouth Scouts

Ellen Sparkes looks on fondly as Exmouth Scouts (left to right) Paul Radgick, ?, ?, David Long and Chris Witkiss, are presented with the Queen's Scout Award by Lord Roborough on 14 April 1976.

Below – 24 July 2009, Exmouth and Budleigh Salterton Explorer Scout group as they set of for their two week trip to Namibia. Back (l-r): James Kelly, Roy Philp, Tom Oldfield, David Cope, Chris Elliott, Henry Wright, Lewis Phillips, Robert Sinden, Richard Tonkin-Dunn, Scott Parnell, Ben Carlsson, Bob Day, Martyn Long. Front: Martin Woodage, Emily Kelly, Max Newing, Harry Snow, Esther Workman, Katie Lock, April Snow and Liam Slough.